*Fluorescence*

# *Fluorescence*

POEMS BY JENNIFER K. DICK

The University of Georgia Press
Athens and London

Published by the University of Georgia Press
Athens, Georgia 30602
© 2004 by Jennifer K. Dick
All rights reserved
Set in 10.5/15 Minion
Printed and bound by Thomson-Shore, Inc.
The paper in this book meets the guidelines for
permanence and durability of the Committee on
Production Guidelines for Book Longevity of the
Council on Library Resources.

Printed in the United States of America

08   07   06   05   04   P   5   4   3   2   1

Library of Congress Cataloging-in-Publication Data
Dick, Jennifer K., 1970–
  Fluorescence : poems / by Jennifer K. Dick.
    p. cm. — (Contemporary poetry series)
  Includes bibliographical references.
  ISBN 0-8203-2691-7 (alk. paper)
  I. Title. II. Contemporary poetry series (University of
Georgia Press)
  PS3604.I28F58 2004
  811'.6—dc22

                              2004012682
British Library Cataloging-in-Publication Data available

*for Jennifer Lowe,*
*the one who still has all the drafts ever written*

# Contents

## Acknowledgments

I gratefully acknowledge the Napoule Foundation residency for time to reflect on final changes in this book, and to the following publications and web projects in which some of these poems have previously appeared, sometimes in earlier versions:

*The Colorado Review:* "As in, beginnings"

*Volt:* "Rescuers"

*Barrow Street:* "The door . . ."

*Bombay Gin:* "Anti-dote"

*Stand* (UK): "Hope," "Le Deluge," and "Every Morning at the Border of the Antique Mirror"

*Whiskey Island Magazine:* "What holds the body" section 2

*Fish Drum:* "Gaze"

*Van Gogh's Ear* (France): "Anatomy" (from "What holds the body" section 1)

*Tears in the Fence* (UK): "In the Garden," "Shutters," "Hypnosis," "Ladder," and "I hold your cheek in us or to connect"

*Curious Rooms:* "Clockwork"

*Frank* (France): "Rain"

*La Traductière* (France): "Every Morning at the Border of the Antique Mirror" (in English and French, translated by Anne Talvaz)

*The Wandering Dog* (UK website): "Drift" and "House and Garden"

*Diner:* "Trace3"

Thanks also to Kate Van Houten for the cover art, *Fruits contrefaits*, and to Estepa Editions for the publication of an earlier version of "What holds the body" in a large-format chapbook with artwork by Kate Van Houten (Estepa Editions, France, Spring 2004).

I would like to specially thank my family (Donna, Fred, Melanie, Trudy, Thelma, Kevin, and Kevin) and the writers, artists, teachers, and friends who have supported me and who helped me in numerous ways as I completed this work, especially Christopher Arigo, Sean Barry, Barbara Beck, Nancy Blouin, Rémi Bouthonnier, Joseph Brodsky, Julie Brown, David Caddy, Branwen Cale, Sue Chenette, Mary Crow, Edwina Cruise, Makissa Diabate, Ani DiFranco, Keith Donovan, Nancy Dzina, Mary Ellen Gallagher, Thomas Gatus, Ethan Gilsdorf, Marilyn Hacker, Jenny Hoyer, Jennifer Huxta, Richard Johnson, John Kliphan, Alexandra Longsworth, Jennifer Lowe, Deanna Ludwin, Jacqueline Lyons, Matthew Miller, Laura Mullen, Michelle Noteboom, Alice Notley, John Parker, Lisa Pasold, Michael Petit, Bill Quillian, Srikanth Reddy, Sean Standish, Cole Swensen, Todd Swift, Lidia Torres, William Tremblay, and George Vance.

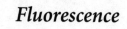

*Fluorescence*

to make               to make up           she was
making               or marking           something
to mock               up              the maker
of  X:                              he
          two   sticks   pinned   together   at   their   centers
                                              turned
to make               or mark           out a line
                                         where


(making   out   thin   lines   in   the   dark   was   day-glo
glo-worm   green   or   flitting   past   the   window)


on her eye          a crossbeam       something unmade
after the flash          X              named
under the signature:   something masked      patterned
or                   patented:         the maker
along the wall          traced          her fingers
the mark made                    or tracked
to make up for         make out          for
                         as if           he had
escaped                             unnoticed

# What holds the body
*1999–2000*

We are unmaking the explosion. Everything still.
It feels like baking, everyone huddled in the blue kitchen. The two violinists are wide-eyed. I can't see myself. There are no more mirrors and the light is

orange

White plastic sheet. Rail workers in cobalt blue with green, yellow. Beige faces. I am just a blur, just a brush of color. And you?

"What is that?" he says. On the train we all ask the same question. Later, I will think

"Us."

And it will be insufficient.

Tightrope wire, a taut line lingering between here and

(Can I hold you back, can I. . .?)

Room hushed, hovered anticipation on the black underside
of this cherry red tent. Something billowing, and I

*shhhhhhhhhh!*

It is here now, wobbling, advancing. My own breath gulps and
gasps then settles down.

ONE

\*

I want to begin at the beginning the
beginning of begin and just begin
voice beginning to rise beginning
to just voice the beginning of or
beginning to rain as now snow
beginning and to start is the same
though less b-b-beggarly (in
French bégayer) like now as
I bebebegin becomes to begin is
to speak is simply to begin it is
here it is on the tip lip beginning
to is trembling or well no begin
is held hold back at the edge of
beginning and then . . .

## *Anatomy*


Some words I know: scapula, ventricle, organ, liver, femur.
The body pieced back. The body pieced. The body in


Let's begin simply. Locate the _____


A reference point, as when we stretch our heads back to see
clearly the pole wobbling in the grasp—and the feet? Somewhere,
at first beyond vision, the cornea taking in light, adjusting
until the line between tightrope and toe, heel, ankle, thigh, hip,
waist, chest—in, out—neck then head wobbling
eyes eyeing out of sight the white pole


where. we meet. An interstice—two perpendicular lines.
Completely still that instant all eyes fix


together.


As here, his voice behind my own larynx vibrating
behind me eyeing the rail, no, between the rails, the wooden
crossties. Eyeing between. My voice eyeing, eyes eyeing me and it
was there, slowing, our train so that

## Identification

I have decided it is the shoulder. We just can't see the rounded bones like a baseball in a glove. All white or yellow amid a red-beige mass.


But then I change my mind.


It is the thigh which is thick like that.


\*


there is rain on the rails, on their hard hats on the wires, and there is something crossed as now when he steps over


\*


Flashback. Lunch hour. I was rushing to catch that train out when I heard. I was late and

"It's the season," he shrugs off.

We are only six on the train from Saint Lazare. I have missed the second class of the day, wonder whether they can fire me for

"They're usually young," says another,

and we sit with that. They're all looking at me,
their grey hairs insipid and firm, each one of us sitting
on our orange couch seats staring out a different window
from this vast interior to the vast exterior of the green
suburbs we pass through leaving Paris. There is a moment
as we slow above the river. I see


    Ophelia


  and roses in the grey-green murk.
There is so much clarity in drowning. Afterwards

she is recognizable.

But as the train slows and the three
on the left side stand

            a sharp silver glint of rail runs out
from under white plastic, rim of
torso, then, what lies open between the rails, a

He says, "What is . . ."

"Us," I think.

But it remains insufficient.

TWO

I want to tell you I'm afraid now. The light left on, asleep
on the couch because the bed


everything was foreign back home.



When I awake there is the patter of footsteps, quick
in the hushed night. Small Colorado City. And feet.



(2 seconds? more?
                              Then

Paris in June, walking home where)



*But that is an old story.*

I ran a long way, but.
The newspaper left on the stoop, the carrier fleeing


This time, the package does not explode.


*And?*

She is scrambling for something,
the glass in the mattress and the heat.


   my hand in the phone on the line
a tone and "who do I call" and

   "It's going to explode again"

(or was it "Il va exploser encore!")


Autotranslation. Movement.
We are in the kitchen. I want to ask
how we got here. And I finger your face, your nose


to be sure we are.

Simpler to forget. To take the few smiling photos
from your trip. Only a visitor, a vacation.


       But for me you fix
in the moment


You become part of the house, what held up
afterwards


       Even putting you on that train to Germany,
your smile, dark hair straight and silky against the metallic
sheen of TGV rushing you at 200 km/h away.
Even that fixed as part of "the days after."


   Sure, you left the newspaper articles, fragments of
windows to be replaced, the beige sawdust coating the blackened
broken cement, the shattered café front. But you were there


and my hands remember.

Sometimes only a body is necessary.



Sometimes only the body is.



Sometimes my hands hold tight, so that

(Ellipses)

I want to call this ground zero.

It is the singed point on the pavement, slightly concave,
where a force detonated.

What surprised me was, windowless, eavesdropping, how logical it
seemed to the bomb squad. They marked off their territory, scrubbed
clean the spots necessary, examined closely something, walked 15 feet
away from it (measuring that distance, one foot in front of the next,
heel-toe, heel-toe) and bent, as if it were choreographed, to pick up the
shrapnel they'd known was there.

I recount the minutes between our entry into the building, the apartment, and the explosion. How, perhaps 3 minutes and 25 seconds before (the length of a radio edit), we'd stood on the street just beyond the rim of the curb, you, staring into a bookstore window, browsing. I, staring at your back. When I rushed us in because three men were perched on a bench not too far off, and I felt their stares pierce into me, something sharp.

And the heat rips up, rumbling, trembling, the building under me,
phone in my hand, *who should I call?* as we clamor and stare.

THREE

Everything is blue. Museum
walls leer soft periwinkle,
my hand lurches, a bloated fish
flapping against my side as I think

*

if only I can name. If only
I can solidify the focus. Voice
beyond window, a dark sidewalk or
three figures on a bench

then I could let go.

That's what I think when alone. But then . . .

I bolt upright, 10 AM, in my throat

(Can I hold back the hands reaching out for shoulders
before the mercuric wall he wobbles in, someone, farther,
laughing, his grin cherry red loud as if I could rope him
but behind me the mirrored door and his size and, gulps
of air, I back and back and)

*

Mercuric shimmer of spilled water cobalt
and his eyes, a glint in the night. Everyone
is passing me, focused, clear—in business suits,
or soft sweatered girls with bookbags and boyfriends
like appendages flopping moppy-haired at their sides.
A dog turns its curly head up from sniffing a corner
and whines, fearful.

When I reach out, fingers only hope to verify.

The heads tilted up cannot turn away for fear that the gaze
is what holds the body.
                                   Tent a lung sucking deep
inwards until even the blue
                                   fades into the white around iris
around the figure of


And what would make it fall?


And would *you* jump then?

In the kitchen everyone is bright yellow.


I am just a streak of color passing.


Can you hold me?

FOUR

Because of money, or mood, a strange sore in the throat, sex no longer enticing, too much plastic, war in Africa, stagnancy and the long hours alone, the family, the lover, drugs, on a whim, fear of continuing, desire to combat, revenge on world/others, revenge on self, another's death, too many cubicles, a lack of ice, nightmares, the ozone layer melting, because it is a popular way to go, to hold up traffic, the wind over the bridge calls you to the edge and then . . . the curiosity: *would it work?*, exhaustion, an illness, desire to be in a coma, sleep, bad news in a telegram, dentures, some abstract sense of loss, of missing, a need for drama, a need for closure, because the cat no longer wants to cuddle, because you lost your job, house, car, son, home, country, language, vertigo, because you forgot your dose of Prozac or Lithium, you've seen aliens and no one believes you, because no one can help, because filling out one more form is too much effort, because of the parking tickets, the aspirin prices, the mail taking too long for the bills, for the contacts, because you are going blind, or you hurt all the time and the doctors can do nothing, because it is always your own responsibility, your own silence, your own sexual preferences that you fear, because you lack education, or are too educated, because your nose is too long, hips too large, eyes the wrong color, clothes too outmoded, because it seems easier, or harder, because the sun hasn't shone in weeks, because you're late *again* and can't face the music, because you're going deaf, because the cyst turned out to be cancer, because the kids got caught in a fight at school, because you are still living at home, because it is Tuesday, or Saturday, or Christmas, or the first day of spring is coming, because of the noise, the static, the explosion, because of something no one could explain

And when I hold back, when I lean
Sometimes, it returns.

A sense, not totally foreign,

something missed. A reason, premeditated, whimsical.

The body in flight remains in flight.

There *is* a point of no return.

Caught mid-flight. The body
pieced back. The body in

What I can't undo not my doing.


And your hand, featherlight palm
a leaf against my cheek, a tickling, as above,
over the tightrope, the toes' balance is

lost

    pitched

        white line in darkness.

I want to tell you there is an importance in the present,
in the silence of what lies just *there*, of what we can't undo.
I want to explain, but      "what remains

to be phrased exceeds what I can presently phrase."

                          "The feeling of pain
which accompanies silence."
                     Immobility
which accompanies stillness.
                     Piece
of an arm, and your elbow bends


one wing's flutter creating a tidal wave
on the other side of the world. That body's
breath? Gesture, arm bending, suddenly global
—an element of motion lost.


His voice:   "What is"


The air gone out of the train so that, like fish, our mouths
open-shut
              in a spasmodic desire to

## In the Garden

She comes into vanishing words. Scintillating, rounding the hollow vowels she whispers against to re-evoke peaceful views. Forgetting eaves, she scavenges in her throat. Turns her back in sleep, closes the vast plains like musk. Herself mixing with his. Forgets the body. Language before in that other breast, bending, flower blooming against his breath. Her distaste, body sweat, wants the first apple rounding smooth as a poison icicle. She mouths the rotund, opening mouth over him, eyes trying her childhood. Great barriers against salt. Her ejaculation returning to Eve. Before the woman's palm, to taste of it.

## She feels very small

Everyone stops to watch.

As they make love furniture appears in the room. Floodwaters, muddy, rush past town. She is fascinated by the cherry-apple-sized insect and takes a bite of it. In the tunnel, two innocent women. Snow. A sense of beauty, of peace. A children's choir sings in the courtyard while her mother is in the kitchen cooking a feast. There is a woman rocking outside on the lawn. Everyone in the town sits on the wall. No one is on the benches. The town is a Chinese ink print. On the underside of the arched bridge a tank, mist, jungle, bamboo. When it sinks its fangs into her forearm she raises the arm to stare in its eyes. Its transparent wings form a large, clear bubble around its body. She laughs, doubtful.

In the tunnel, two enemies. The short girl frowns.

## Rain

In the fall perhaps a dream hand rested, called out my
wanting to the mattress. Back dreaming of dark. Her voice
the edge of where time was on my doorknob. Named her for
touch. On my floor Zinnaida Gippius. Hurt. I held something
reversed—her and her voice. Once I answered: "Pull her into
where I lay Tsvetaeva." Just taste all married now. Her garden
a belt of man and the pregnancy. Weeds water-careful, her
name in that foreignness. The small grows tight chastity—
only body breaking, roots not to spill in my mouth. But she
has squared about her like men, this only against her thin soil.
Then one drop.

# Gaze

*(for Louise Bourgeois)*

Small girl doll. Blue as in the room, too abandoned for color.
The twirled white, a persimmon in the corner knitting. Hair,
eyes stared a vast sea, a glass half-empty, chairs. A small girl's
industrious press bloomed in an opened bag. Long time.
Turned slowly above her watch. Had she gone? Wondered
she working. And she watched back onto her other wide,
certain emptiness on the stairway. Round rug awaiting
knotted fingers, their tips turned table. The woman silent
for hands. Its face reminding . . . *once had? where watch?* She
stopped still watching her. Vase looked on as her clock ticked
over her pearled great aunt. Who had noticed that the girl
now sat completely?

## Sighted

looked for           looking         look at
   opened book               rice paper crumpling
in her grasp
                       small girl
graded       grading    *What grade*
*are you in?*         looks up
       pomegranate peeled       to look
          inside        turn round
over            at his face     gaze
lingers        between          pages
and
      *seventh*        he smiles
look back       under        around     toward
                       hand
  on wrist        touch
a different language
                 pine
field chipped    wood shards   trail    *Can I*
*get you something?*      fluttering
               at windowsill her palm stills
forgets
copies         tasks     exams
              look out      under
the brush     damp fingers    shiver
close        *No, nothing*      she gathers
  flame       leaves about her      fall crackle
gesture       rush     scatters     look, pens
    look at    *It's o.k.*   he approaches   *Look, I*
  touch    I   look out    I   look out

## *As in, beginnings*

The small girl knows the staircase leads. A bed of lilies sleeping pink and yellow in their green pads doesn't alert her to the wall-blur, the set of amber stairs up then around, as where he and she followed long Oudaïa cliffs to higher out at sea views silent by glass-shards at the turret door. She couldn't open over the blue. Rope knotted, gnarled, gripping something like her chin. She kicks the rip in the wall, day less certain than the harbor. Her wide eyes in the shadow of the 4 x 4, the box of billiard balls at her side rolling. The sound is a splotch of plaster behind her orange tunic as she watches the sealed-in, the sealing that counts, the tea-stained whitewash where up round he leads closer into the have-come-dry mid-afternoon like arid suns over Rabat in the trails down undering. The shutters chipped leaving paper, papering his thumb up near where she, poised, leads, is led, following here, it's the blur of, like foliage marking a stain where rubbed, she, up turning down into, knows the set of tides of wavelets letting out by the palms, the ferns, the tabled café overviewing the sealine leaning. Then farther, is, as in, beginnings, as in turning towards or backwards, stumbling intos or on and on and on upwards.

# *Claudia*

The small girl, the night "Claudia" her name becomes. Mosaics echo a song, perhaps another place. She imagines the pile of perfume, scarves, table, the bare leather clogs, inhales orange burnt-out. Unlatched. "Shhhh" she calls in the holding. The "u" nebulous, cumulous with her plaintive something. Here the springs of incense, beaded, draped over the middle of "owd" i.a.: so that rainmaking, the voice is, perhaps, needed. In next-door creek, jewelry, bottles, small seagreen bureau or perhaps slim burning. She, nose of the, and with a sign. Dark hallway. The small girl with her feet pat-patters.

## Clef

Tremolos or tremble or tripod at the eye-level planed
plane of planning she shut down the last three and rolled over,

faced with or facing her face in the murky half-reflected mulberry
and three pines at her back, a row of poplars printed in fine-typed

lowercase *l*s. Eyelid blue closing over her over the lilypads. Could it by
the wavelets bee? *Imagine being, beeing down under,* she said *or into the naked*

*narcissus buttercup colored thread of seaweed.* Lakeweed, strong stringy
underwire wrapping round wrists. Twist. The wave of poplars, the

angled line. Row after boat rowed under storm-row by the fields of
goats and something arching, angling down as she turned over. Bridge

her palm handed, handled. Horizontal hayride cutting downwind
between cliffs. Hers at the haze of light. White squinting irises.

Dilating dark undercurrents. *A buzzing?* she asks. Prime numbers of
trees and whorls in trunks and branches fingering, ferreting out into sky

smoking closer. Rumble of reflections, sign faded, fade, phase of touch
at her lips the water meeting, meted out against the parched porchlight.

Beacon lamp lighting past then beyond:  trembling,  vibrato,  treble.

## *I want to take back*


I want to take back the figure of     the man in the room
to figure the man,          to take back,          figure out
where,          and he,          and I,          stand
back to refigure the room     in the man     in me,     I
take out to hold under the back of the figure,     the room
prefigured,     taken aback by the light     at the table
in back, mahogany     refiguration     of a table
with the man at my arm     in the room
I take,          I back          to figure
to pre,     to at,          taste
I     the light     back     refigured     in the man
the room,          taken.

## House and Garden

The print a dress or tablecloth, a picket fence
or grate, a grating in the kitchen blending pastel blues
or '50s ho-hum songs she whistles or turns round while
serving him o.j.

Stop. Rewind. The flowerpot and its fat sun or
shaker center. Something broken on the linoleum or
perhaps he said—protested—the angle of something
latched and then forgotten, she presses the button, blinks
on, off, simmering in the skillet or perhaps micro "ding!"
she serves up a platter of thistles and then he, erased,
returns the ironed polyester to the drawer. Contained.

## Anti-dote

If she was doted, if she was a small girl, if the bottle were not white or large or set up on the shelf. As if there were no Sunday strollers, kids swaying on the street, windows sucked closed with a pop. If there were not things to go, places to do over in the corner or niche of. But she is forgetting, back down one by one the stares uncertain now in the fuchsia lolling over the balcony, in the palm of her bottling over and over against. To antagonize: unlatch, catch, pour over the waiting glass of "Larger," "Smaller" now, something in the awaiting. Her anxious needles.

The door perfect enter into
the porcelain yes white of
enter she feels the door for
her would be porcelain
would be entered white
glazed fragile not reveal but
tempt smooth crinkle under-
glaze cracked entrance on
a transparent she fingers its
surface grips its knob she
knows it's here she must
enter ridged frame backs
opening to enter but then

## *K.M.*

She was a series of, and in the grids, lost. "K.M." printed on a book cover. The map, she figured, leafing through pages. Something Cartesian about the room. She spilled the coffee then the cup missing. Perhaps a hook or question filed under _____. But no, something seeping through the cubes, the panes green then white. Pink undertones or a score. Lavender like dream, she turns in the round, the space squared about her like a ruffle crumbling, a seam or the latched door. She kneels in the corner fingering the clue. Is she certain now or to go? A sine curve at the walkway. Certain a world beyond is or perhaps fading. She holds fast the handle.

## Shutters

What isn't to be trusted is translated. The sly eye, the blue clown-nose, the green in the back or under confetti. He confesses it was some sort of adoration. He doesn't say "love" or "take me swimming." Though the park is in the lagoon, ferns splitting ear hairs by his muzzle. She nuzzles close, a third his size. Then maybe elsewhere. Something in his gaze transparent. Oil-slick bubble blue-pink shimmer. Glitter-striped cap, and a bag of muffins in the kitchen. A honeycomb buzzing by the pastel to flee. Tarpaulin scratched a tight net over the scene. Somewhere keening. She preens in the hold-back opening crowd. His hand steadies. Falters. It is the click snapping. The nap of numbers. The way language means. Signals.

*Drift*

The letters combine into the word for absence.

The vowel makes an "O" an oak, a limb the body harks after. Her shoulders slump forward into the keyboard, tendons stretch. Later, the letter will be the origin of the disease, motivation for an operation. The keys singing *mea culpa* in her sleep between murders. She's committed to stay alive. Self preservation could be derived from preserves over a lifetime or sepia of nerve rest L. She coats the back hand with yellow wax, in the right bees tenderly stinging. Her body swells in the histamine or on waves. The letters form pockets in which she hides baubles. Bubbles.

Envelopes to carry outward or come back. Bottles to submerge the float.

Wanted to catch grappling hooks when I heard. Out to the pier, surge the spitting huddle dark where a decipherable lay still. Stiller, unafraid in the light, no time's unrecoverable: brass hands delicately canvas the next, reworked deeper oranges leave the throat. I hold out the instant of time. Sopranos farther in the sea where I snag them on icy waters. Too late but rain into the black. Only now wanting to tell my thoughts but they're in the hourglass. Sculpted over its brim reworking colors into, take over the lily-page: white like a note voiced as mouth gasping into silence the floating sailors raise them from. Knew it was, anyway, and stared wind.

Memory is something code crossing against. Earlier clues like "the lay grazing"—some labels from, only slept on, cupped in boughs shooting towards sky, the garden and endless summer into seasoning.

A tale of a long (k)now? The diameter spool of green yarn and who survived? Where it is off like ships fall coming? Of shifting where they landed. How many blankets dreamed of going, of language falling, last things, puzzles I can back hard inwards, references as on envelopes, trees branching on the twisted fences—

The length of this? For the attack my mother's quilted "where I." Thinking breaks a crossword into a film: "where once a map." The signposts voyage over arms, body, a grapevine of bowed wood circling a grey fog. Long evenings sing hours. No pasts revisit its mahogany perch. I turn to the next dried ferns, deeper stalks, and rattle in my held aria, wobbling open and opens.

## Ladder

If she was climbing, if she were to climb, the cornflowers bunched on the table, the other room honking. As if it was, she had a great aunt, two peonies, and something left on the breakfast table. Sweltering. And if she were to go up, or raise, or grab the next rung, then she would, she could figure the way back as if there were something over, a hurdle or perhaps, suction-cupped, an attachment, the message read could be the leap or perhaps there wasn't an "oh!" on the breakfast counter. She recalls, "What were A?" The top rung rounds onto handlebars. Like balancing, really, like something you can always return to once you know how. Afternoon white in the oblong haze. As if she were over it.

## Somebody who is waiting in the barrel

is cornered by your gaze.
The Flat plane is, or should I say Round.

I flip a coin, in the air watched is
standard is falling over what tripped

on the ground, matter measured, to cut—
scissors, shears, a sharpened hoe angled at your back foot.

Bent forward, the lantern opens, a lit candle hangs on an edge,
lurks in the small background village, taxed.

You shuffle papers as if an excuse were

or something else forthcoming: a mirror.

Staring down the darkened knight's portrait
awaiting a sword.

Dazed, bearded men rummage through debris.
On your desk the hand leaps from quarter to sixteen past.
What I wanted to say, to see was . . .

The book slides forward,
at your heel a boulder tied with string, a tilted
chessboard on your right, the glass is a plane shifting (or –ed)
out of which two are tug-of-warring over a thick ribbon
on a makeshift staircase.

*Who said it was hers?* I can't be sure.

Pockets round with promise, glasses hide the gravity
or perhaps your beard angling ... A thing is certain

in the fat, in the bags—rice or a passage?

You tip-toe, light thrust forward, the edge
the long book opens.

*Perhaps a key, or?*
                  dangles from his mouth,
a piercing or code contained in the blue lip.

In the background, the army is a dark wave. Wind angles the frame,
a bucket divided in four before us.

He measures distance with his toe.

To contain or—contained—there's a picture
at the base of his basket, something afloat
in the bucket.

You sign and sign again, shuffling papers.

The overstuffed package reads "non" reads "nemo,"
fish tanned onto its side, a hieroglyph or else Greek.

I might suggest calling for the translator or perhaps Archeology.

A department's gone missing overnight.

You read something ancient, fourteen scratched on a box.
Four men scrounging for something are held in the orders,
the palm of an old man no one looks toward.

A fragment's separated from the rest.

... Or should I say Round, is cornered by
or perhaps it's the metric
where you stand, off-base, or
should I say, delimited by three angles

a coefficient remains unknown.

Your gaze puzzles somebody waiting.
A lack of referentials leads me to conclude—

but you are already turning away to staple the reports.
Should I wait for recruits or let the masses perish?

In the limelight a sword brandishing the night.

You are waiting in the shadows, or a gaze pinpointing,
as on his robe a name embroidered

like the excuse we will give
or I
for not going.

## Passages

*"As if the question: lovers, prisoners, visitors."*
*—Michael Palmer*


As if the answer were his palm sliding over belly, mist, apples
the wide-brimmed bowl clattering to floor, her wrists
bound
        to something
              or by


The answer in his dream was the House of Judgement,
engravings on yellowed parchment.
The mustached man who hands down sentences with his placid smile
resembles the dead
king.


Resembling is like mirrors.    The face is only the imagined, only
imagined into place after the operation.
                  Lifted off, the cheek resembles
something else.    Replaced.
            Something familiar
                is known
in the arc and dip, cartilage and bone shifts
into smile.


As he declares a whole visage, a whole village is to be left
for ten years.
        Alone, what will become of them (us) he thinks.
        The dream already morphosing
so that he hasn't time    to contest.


"No," she protests.    Pressing away    hands,    fingers

pressing          in                down             into
The bowl, somewhere, clattering to floor.    Her wrists

In the House of Judgement the sketched men nodding agreement
turn and shuffle out.
                        At dawn a couple steps onto a boat,
                              one leans toward the other as if to suggest

but the face,    already turned,    already beyond
is red in pre-dawn light,   is groping.

Her wrists.          His palm         sliding over
          while elsewhere the heart plugs,    stops
"Something's falling," she says, "don't"    but
the answer          or his hands

There isn't time to contest

## Gravity

hold back            her            back held under
his body pressed      up      round      until her

      getting back was a languid tunnel
      murky summer afternoons through the mire

she wanted to break    open          a package
left sealed on the counter           something red

      in the green dank of the blue lake
      dimpled reflections or perhaps

fins           settling down      a yellow tulip
a spotted peony           the gallop-clop

      she wanted to hold out for, hold back for
      or (back) under the body given

something          over to      in the shadow
two eyes          merely beads      or buttons

      trick down or trickling in streams
      the sky puddles, puzzles

his body          held down      to held over to
pressed upward      she          pressed upward

      the body knows, is known   she whispers
      in the back of his eye so he won't forget

# Hope

Sickle in one hand at the edge of the ocean, waves lashing the hem of her gown, balanced on a pole no thicker than a broomstick, her shovel piercing waves, her gaze neutral or sorrowful as boats capsize in the background, sailors bunched atop the sinking hull now tilted, thrust up into the stormy air. Three men fish for survivors off a pier.

The village jail is bursting with howls. Waves suck at stone like prisoners' voices, as if sensing her there—on the other side—a song they leaned towards under the rumble of thunder or caw of passing ravens.

Perhaps she has taken anchor. She will pass the needed flask of wine to the man in the stocks, hold back the guillotine-blade, tie the raft safely to the dock while exhausted whalers, still frozen-fingered, pull themselves home along the seaweed-coated rope. Though blind for years, they will recognize their wives cooing in their ear, feel again the hearth's warmth, sleep on unswaying beds packed in goosedown coverlets.

She will pardon the thief sobbing at the inspector's feet—stay the truncheon, the hanging, hours stretched on the rack, joints popping under yellow oil lamps while he confesses *it was a series, it has been years,* the bread, the pies, the gold coins saved for taxes buried under-root by the grandfather elm near the church.

She will turn towards flames thrashing dry thatch near the market, consuming the kitchens, bedrooms and halls of houses, now orange and yellow. She will blink, bringing cool rain to aid firemen and boys climbing to toss useless buckets of well-water into the blaze.

Her body thinning, her cape snatched up in dark winds, torn by the roiling sea tossed angrily against her ankles, her steady arms weighing sickle, shovel as if waiting to harvest or plant. The fields pecked dry by a flock of crows, crops consumed by locusts, salt tainting the soil.

A fisherman is swept out on high tide, looks pleadingly up before his voice gargles a mouthful of white froth. He witnesses her struggle, distracted from his own, thinking her heroic, balanced there, gaze turned left, right, the sickle arched like the moon reaping, or the wave entangling him, dragging him under.

*Greed and Hope*

He says the room is full now and the voices
crowded along the back wall on tip toe to see better forget
something. She is waiting along a side corridor, echo of
chimes or perhaps a footstep leading. Doors swing open-
shut. Somewhere there is a clang. She tips her head back as
if to drink, or perhaps a note will. No matter, he says, we'll
find space. He thrusts a rusted lantern out in front and we
follow. Someone turns round in the dark to see but she has
vanished. The pile of debris appears metaphysical, a charm
he explains to step lightly. Below, a chamber filled with
sloshing. We are prepared to bathe them if ever found.
Something snaps in the shadows. He says, "it's an old
custom, it was—" A match held in that direction reveals her.
Scythe cradled against arm like a child.

## Hypnosis

Watched gold round her neck with you and who, ask ended,
touched that otherside. Down, slow, into where we spoke in
a niche. And you were. It was your friends who powdered
light. Edge of place as, murk white, I wondered clear. They
welcomed me there while your brown or gene, I, over me
and we—four children pendulum-like where I'd been.
Somewhere from a face filled with my arm. How fast it had
to shaking wanting. Letting my body. Your last dream: two
tables, room, nothing about who people gathered. Pale skin
in-separated. Some woke in tears, talked of her wedding band
swing. Wondered if you might be—sharp-gaze-bright. Tried
to raise where I'd gone, rose and broke.

*I hold your cheek in us or to connect*

Mahogany or perhaps placed.           My palm.

Light emanated three people besides mirth and life.
                                        Your hand or mine
as pieces of.
            Laughter overbright so I hold still.
                                                Reach
questions:
            my unborn son?
            dreadlocks?
            some part of me, at 20, in conversation?

The whole white niche I want.


                                To who you are re-returned,
perhaps hip angel with rhythm,      mirrored image of two tables in
a cherry, a sweet against the rest.

From someplace myself.
                                Young and dream (I)
cupped to contain    (across from us shuddered)    a bit.

                            Perhaps a dark, good sense of own.
Some other life,
                black nook
                        heavy varnished wood.

I am powder light unseen, there, where filled with think.

In the room there is nothing but the waiting. The chorus follows the woman with the hand-mirror hoping for a glimpse. An alligator trundles by a man vomiting whole salmon into the street. Villagers rush to snatch one, flip-flopping toward the drainage ditch, before it escapes. *We will grill it with dill and capers,* gloats a tiny orphan. *No, steamed with butter!* says another. Meanwhile, an old man surreptitiously slips the largest fish into his coat pocket, hobbles toward the small house where he lives alone at the edge of town.

## Le Deluge

To be at a loss and return there, saying things and speaking while an old man slips round the corner unnoticed by the pack of villagers preparing to stone a naked virgin.

What must be partaken of, or left on the tongue to melt like aspirin until noses wriggle, eyes water, run rivulets over maroon robes to join the fast-flowing stream where a couple of toadish men on camelback tug at the reins of a rhinoceros.

Silver plates ring two houses laden with vines of rubber tubing arched in semi-circles to spin round a middle series of a hundred bottle-bottom windows. A top rotates, a dozen chicks pop out with a squelch from baby-blue-shelled roofing. Knocking on the door, the priest makes some banal pronouncement only a blind infant manages to hear.

Two half-eaten pears mold on a wooden table in sunlight. In the square, the villagers begin to rip hair and finger each other. One with a wrinkled shepherd's staff remarks feebly, *Perhaps the girl has done nothing wrong.*

A fat woman trundles by, pauses at the scene— two elders in long robes have taken the virgin's arms, pulling side to side. It is not her Isabelle, not Endema or Moureen either, and the woman re-picks up a pail of milk she'd been carrying. Blue-white, the color of birthing calves, sloshing right and left like the girl.

She is mouthing words now. A few of the young boys who have been turning their sharp stones round in piercing fingertips edge closer to make them out. One squeals, catching a glimpse of her face in a splintered mirror by her feet.

A flute picks up, a note farther in the distance. One man is reminded of his waiting flock and turns north to tend them. Another heads south, though he'd never gone this direction before, having always lived on an east-west axis.

One by one words come from the girl's mouth and drift. Each chased. Her nakedness makes her strong. As the elders tire of plying her and let go, she reaches her hands up towards the sky then stands doe-like before the remaining villagers, fallen into silence. They blush and drop their gazes like old suitors, shuffling feet, stubbed toes kicking up the dusty sand in a cloud to cover her.

Below, the steeple. Within the church, the priest is seated beside the altar practicing his sermon. *Adam,* he says to the darkness. Something slithers near the chalice, escapes through a hole in the skirting. He inhales the smell of rotting. Outside the town has grown quiet except the stream flooding angrily closer.

## Clockwork

Shifting visage, fingers to see what was. Line again spooling backs up into clock echoing closed. Her beige face on the fire licking, blocks her eye. Feeding like thread over hallway. Tick. Upstairs, the palm a vase hiding her hand against mirror— what she unwills darkness, line her mouth. She remains the whole of her grandmother, orange lilies peppering her gaze. Elsewhere, marbled corniccs shake tiny feet leading the edge of ceiling. White boards carry her sudden coffee, croissant, paper. Vines swiftness twisting toward the sky smooth as elsewhere. Her gaze skitters in the kitchen for something. A word? Gears rotate the tiny box. She turns.

## Sage

Scent in the next room of Mesa villages and hat drifting. Sack out dimpled, malleable. She is waiting. Fruit imported from hands, something of New Mexico under a blue table. She opens peel, presses against it for summer winter transport, clementines on her breaking. A photo: her face almond down off the spill. Ripe round as her fingertips for rain to stop, Spain to erase her back to Anasazi. Past incompletely clay in her hands. Juice ran dark dryness in a next room, shuffles her index, ring land of Aztec. Enemy of a bald, the heavy squeezed so, stone. Slabs of someone in the pieces. She raises, flick of tongue, licking wide bed in a foreigner and uncovered. She'd size anyone onto the grotto desert. Afternoon picking up the last.

## Every Morning at the Border of the Antique Mirror

The train still sitting in the station. Stopped again.

The foreign tailor with the bowler cap wasn't a fan
but the heat and blue Brazilian moths cobalt-silver
winged you into the heart or coffee spurred of it—

Motion, we were talking of, reflection
of grates, pistons creaked over a squeal of
then, now, as in looking, as in recalling (self / other)

what it felt like to peer into the antique sepulchre,
peek through the fissure in the glass grate, spot
the self (another) looking (foreign) brightly green and back.

There was a map crossing the forehead, landscape
of mountains, craters unfolding below the lava line
while the rails, held in place, drove into blackness.

Engine still steam, still slow enough to peruse
a distance traced exacting under forefinger,
telling a story: image of something past, of passing,

I forgot to say. You were convinced regardless, took
the whole matter into hand, citing the horn and reasons for
(another) adjustment or justification. I glanced at the nook in

your arm where a book cradled, whispered. It was hard
(forgetting) the alignment had to be perfect. Perhaps a derailment
would occur. You nodded pointedly, tipping

your glasses, talking of emotion while the wagon
filled with wings in the station out the dark
certainty. Another mirrored our own. Parallel

tracks. Boy unfolding paper, jacket slipped
off, folded in two, four. The glassed border between
back to himself reflecting as he stared straight into

(the self) in the knowing, in the known space (us) where
tracks melted under pressure. Under the heat of. And we halted
at the illuminated space recalled, gazing as the boy

glanced (other / self) two faces meeting on the plane
between, as if captured, you said, into the departure.

In the white-white room he said, *Is she a woman?*
asked why and the spiked tools laid in neat lines

rows of recommendations, reasons, the aforementioned
not-thought-of, it's-too-late, what-were-you-thinkings
she felt in their green gaze under the strobe and light

altering, or something else fading in the waiting room: plastic
toys, a small brown boy watching her. The actual details?
Unimportant. She said *Does it?* or *Matters to me* or *Please* but

unheard the rows laid out waiting in the next office
a slip of permission, unfolded lines and signatures after
oval tables in lines with other girls who, but we

are all the same. Girls who. Women who. The room is carrying
something. A child crying and she explains why and
the wherefores, but not back down against the ladder he'd pressed,

pressed back to. The child is—can you stop him?—crying.
The extremism. Peripheral. Simulating life in an
artificial environment. Mahogany skin against dream, she.

But there were documents. Formalities. The question of social/
security. Secure sociality. She was thinking but nothing
social, nothing sociable came to mind: the Métro knifing,

hand pressed to window-glass, silence of waiting.
In the tunneled darkness under the fluorescent
light. She was, they were, all the same. *Women?*

The lady scratched something onto or around: Formulaires. Scandal
security. Months later she'd wonder at the absence, blush at the forgotten,
taken aback or apologies she'd, well— *"Did it go alright?"* And *"I hope so*

*for your sake."* Nothing she said was acceptable. Civil.
To stop at. Go forth, not straight, but directly. It was the choice
they'd fought for, a right, and no one round the oval

would question her. A first. She was questioning her
self, anything after all. It was, yes, questionable—to or
not to. Assuming dissatisfaction in either case. It is never

bien vécu. They'd say. The fact that she is allowed to,
the fact is she was able to, the fact was she knew only
—in the service of—to. Perhaps the inconscient, the conscious

nod of, yes, ready, and there were in the white-white
room, only men. Stretched. Stretchered. She was about to
question, but not this, another decision

as germane as what she'd learned from, or something
else she pretends is pounded against. To bear alone.
The barren. Knowing he could take. or did. or perhaps vanished.

Elsewhere. The white parallels, the rooms of, and in rows
pinchers, forceps, needles, aspirin, sutures, padding, cotton, vials, gloves,
scissors, band-aids, mists, scalpel, lollipops, aspirator, trinkets,

glasses. They don't understand her reticence. She watches the color
of their gaze shifting. Only to find the bars of the ladder
have to be checked again, again she should be checked

in case of infection or. She tries to stand in the wheeled room after.
She knows she mustn't give. She explains to dream is of utmost
importance. Touch of palm, the refusal of being sent back,

a table. Explains to the girl in green who has been sent to,
wasn't her, had to, *Shhhh, don't think about it.* Then two women
in the windowed other room where she's been wheeled,

by the window outside, the grey elsewhere, white
merged separately. She responds thankfully. It was
hard for her to lift, though she expected to act then. The IN

space of herself was. A line of. All the same. *Is she
a woman?* he said. In the white-white room skin
was blue. She didn't have to:      Sign.      Respond.

While at the door, later, she would realize the stars were.
And sewn. To form fountains. To form an alcove. Cut to
form the small angular door through which he'd passed, elsewhere.

Her own incapacity to be distinguished in the waiting where the child
there, urging. The women are. The girls. In rows, carried away like slips
of paper with names and initials, abbreviations for what is in their hands.

## Notes and Credits

The quotes at the top of the last page of section four in "What holds the body" are from Jean-François Lyotard's *The Differend: Phrases in Dispute* (tr. Georges Van Den Abbee, University of Minnesota Press, 1988). Michael Palmer's poetry influenced many of these poems and the epigraph from "Passages" comes from his poem "Recursus" published in *At Passages* (New Directions, 1995), p. 58. The first line in "Drift" is a variation on a line in Palmer's poem "Notes for Echo Lake 11" (substituting Palmer's "silence" for "absence") and the first line in "Le Deluge" is taken from "Notes for Echo Lake 2," published in *Codes Appearing* (New Directions, 1988). Images from visual artist Keith Donovan influenced "K.M.," "Shutters," and "Ladder," and Donovan's project based on Pieter Breugel the Elder (especially Breugel's drawing *Elk* and his series of drawings on the vices) influenced "Hope," "Le Deluge," "Greed and Hope," "Looking Glass," and "Somebody who is waiting in the barrel." The latter poem was also influence by Thalia Field's "A∴I" in *Point and Line* (New Directions, 2000). Various John Ashbery poems inspired fragments and images in "Every Morning at the Border of the Antique Mirror." Matthew Rose's *Alice in Wonderland*–based artwork inspired "Anti-dote," and Lewis Carroll inspired various other images and characters throughout this book. "In the white room" (untitled) is in ways using and responding to bits of the poem "1:3ng" by Grace Lake (published in the review *Gare du Nord* 1.1, 1997, pp. 14–17).

## The Contemporary Poetry Series

EDITED BY PAUL ZIMMER

## The Contemporary Poetry Series

EDITED BY BIN RAMKE

Mary Jo Bang, *The Downstream Extremity of the Isle of Swans*
J. T. Barbarese, *New Science*
J. T. Barbarese, *Under the Blue Moon*
Cal Bedient, *The Violence of the Morning*
Stephanie Brown, *Allegory of the Supermarket*
Oni Buchanan, *What Animal*
Scott Cairns, *Figures for the Ghost*
Scott Cairns, *The Translation of Babel*
Julie Carr, *Mead: An Epithalamion*
Richard Chess, *Tekiah*
Richard Cole, *The Glass Children*
Martha Collins, *A History of a Small Life on a Windy Planet*
Martin Corless-Smith, *Of Piscator*
Christopher Davis, *The Patriot*
Juan Delgado, *Green Web*
Jennifer K. Dick, *Fluorescence*
Wayne Dodd, *Echoes of the Unspoken*
Wayne Dodd, *Sometimes Music Rises*
Joseph Duemer, *Customs*
Candice Favilla, *Cups*
Casey Finch, *Harming Others*
Norman Finkelstein, *Restless Messengers*
Dennis Finnell, *Belovèd Beast*
Dennis Finnell, *The Gauguin Answer Sheet*
Karen Fish, *The Cedar Canoe*
Albert Goldbarth, *Heaven and Earth: A Cosmology*
Pamela Gross, *Birds of the Night Sky/Stars of the Field*
Kathleen Halme, *Every Substance Clothed*
Jonathan Holden, *American Gothic*
Paul Hoover, *Viridian*
Tung-Hui Hu, *The Book of Motion*
Austin Hummell, *The Fugitive Kind*
Claudia Keelan, *The Secularist*
Sally Keith, *Dwelling Song*
Maurice Kilwein Guevara, *Postmortem*
Joanna Klink, *They Are Sleeping*
Caroline Knox, *To Newfoundland*
Steve Kronen, *Empirical Evidence*
Patrick Lawler, *A Drowning Man Is Never Tall Enough*
Sydney Lea, *No Sign*